CRITTERS

(AND THE CHURCH)

THREE EMPERORS
(AND THE CHURCH)

Aaron Erhardt

ERHARDT PUBLICATIONS
Louisville, Kentucky
2014

FOREWORD

The story of the church of Christ is not fictional; but rather, it reveals the real history of the people of God, chosen by Christ through obedience to the gospel. Thus, the church began at a real historical time and place (Acts 2), with real events transpiring all around her. The culture into which the church was born, and the influence wielded by the authorities in power, dictated the experiences of our brothers and sisters in Christ of the first several centuries. In writing about three of the emperors who made decisions and took action that touched the lives of so many Christians, Aaron Erhardt has done a great service for those of us who care about the church from its inception until now.

With the writing of *Three Emperors,* Aaron continues to produce books that are unique to him and his style of teaching. The book is precise in its history, having been meticulously researched, and clear in its delivery. In other words, in keeping with the tradition of books penned by Aaron Erhardt, *Three Emperors* is both scholarly and easy to read and understand.

The three emperors about whom Aaron writes — Nero, Domitian, and Constantine — are all fascinating in their own way. To read about their lives and (at least with the first two) their reckless insanity, and then to think of Christians forced to live under their tyranny, is not only very interesting, but also provocative. Can you imagine having a President framing Christians with evil doings just to promote his own cause, or sponsoring a country wide persecution against God's people? Aaron does a good job in describing these emperors engaged in such activity and the consequences for the disciples of Christ. His work with Constantine, though, is especially worth the read. Finally, we have a writer who realizes that this emperor was no saint. Yes, the church prospered physically because of his edict, but spiritually was led deeper into apostasy. Knowing Aaron the way I do, his will always elevates the spiritual over the physical, the soul over the flesh, and his writings about Constantine are in keeping with that trait.

I commend this good book to all who are interested in the history of the church. It is a part of church history that is not often written about, but is very important nevertheless. This book is a good addition to the growing number of outstanding books that can be found within "Erhardt Publications."

Don Wright

DEDICATION

To a mother and her son,

Renee Burns

Kenny Burns II

They remind me of a modern-day
Eunice and Timothy, with their great faith
and sincere love.

TABLE
OF CONTENTS

INTRODUCTION

Christianity came about in the days of the Roman Empire. This proved to be a very difficult environment for Christians, who were soon labeled "atheists" for not worshipping the Roman gods (including the emperor) and "cannibals" for observing the Lord's Supper. They were also accused of disrupting business for preaching against animal sacrifices and gross immorality for professing to love their "brothers" and "sisters," which people assumed was sensual.

The initial persecution suffered by Christians was not state-sponsored. It was the result of local backlash at the hands of Jews and pagans. The book of Acts records the

"progression of aggression" from verbal threats (4:21) to physical beatings (5:40) and then murder (7:58). Things escalated from there. A regional king who was eager to please the Jews killed James and imprisoned Peter (12:1-5). Paul was threatened at Iconium (14:6), was stoned at Lystra (14:19), was beaten

Nero

at Philippi (16:23), and was rioted against at Thessalonica, Berea, Ephesus, and Jerusalem (17:5, 13; 19:28; 21:30).

The first emperor to actively persecute the church was Nero in A.D. 64. He blamed Christians for setting fire to Rome in order to remove mounting suspicion from himself.

> **"Consequently, to get rid of the report, Nero fastened the guilt and inflicted the most exquisite tortures on a class hated for their abominations, called Christians by the populace. Christus, from whom the name had its origin, suffered the extreme penalty during the reign of Tiberius at the hands of one of our procurators, Pontius Pilatus, and a most mischievous superstition, thus checked for the moment, again broke out not only in Judaea, the first source of the evil, but even in Rome, where all things hideous and shameful from every part of the world find their centre and become popular. Accordingly, an arrest was first made of all who pleaded guilty; then, upon their information, an immense multitude was convicted, not so much of the crime of firing the city, as of hatred against mankind. Mockery of every sort**

was added to their deaths. Covered with the skins of beasts, they were torn by dogs and perished, or were nailed to crosses, or were doomed to the flames and burnt, to serve as a nightly illumination, when daylight had expired. Nero offered his gardens for the spectacle, and was exhibiting a show in the circus, while he mingled with the people in the dress of a charioteer or stood aloft on a car. Hence, even for criminals who deserved extreme and exemplary punishment, there arose a feeling of compassion; for it was not, as it seemed, for the public good, but to glut one man's cruelty, that they were being destroyed" (*Annals,* 15:44).

"When Nero, finding that his conduct was greatly blamed, and a severe odium cast upon him, determined to lay the whole upon the Christians, at once to excuse himself, and have an opportunity of glutting his sight with new cruelties. This was the occasion of the first persecution; and the barbarities exercised on the Christians were such as even excited the commiseration of the Romans themselves. Nero even refined

upon cruelty, and contrived all manner of punishments for the Christians that the most infernal imagination could design. In particular, he had some sewed up in skins of wild beasts, and then worried by dogs until they expired; and others dressed in shirts made stiff with wax fixed in axletrees, and set on fire in his gardens, in order to illuminate them" (*Foxe's Book of Martyrs,* pp. 12-13).

Christians had a shady reputation in Rome. They were regarded by many as members of a subversive organization. This made them an easy scapegoat for Nero. While we do not know how many Christians died at that time, the torture they endured was intense.

Jesus, who suffered persecution Himself, taught that His followers would be persecuted. He said, "Blessed are you when others revile you and persecute you and utter all kinds of evil against you falsely on my account. Rejoice and be glad, for your reward is great in heaven, for so they persecuted the prophets who were before you" (Matthew 5:11-12). Paul added, "Indeed, all who desire to live a godly life in Christ Jesus will be persecuted" (2 Timothy 3:12). Christians are called upon to endure persecution regardless of the consequences (Revelation 2:10).

"Eighty and six years have I served him, and he never once wronged me; how then shall I blaspheme my King, Who hath saved me?"

Polycarp
to the proconsul

Stephen (Acts 7:58), James (Acts 12:2), and Antipas (Revelation 2:13) are specifically named as martyrs in Scripture. Tradition says that Paul was beheaded, Peter was crucified upside down, and Thomas was stabbed with a spear. In fact, John was the only apostle who was not executed, though he was exiled to Patmos (Revelation 1:9). John described Rome at the end of the first century as "drunk with the blood of the saints, the blood of the martyrs of Jesus" (Revelation 17:6; also see 18:24). Blood continued to spill in the second and third centuries. Two of the most notable martyrs of that time were Ignatius and Polycarp.

Christianity was fueled by the blood of its saints. Attempts to eradicate the church backfired, as the martyrs loomed larger than the murderers. Choosing to "die rather than deny" was a powerful testimony that led more and more people to the Lord.

Though state-sponsored persecution of Christians was sporadic in the Roman Empire, there were plenty of emperors who did take such action (Nero, Domitian, Trajan, Marcus Aurelius, Septimius Severus, Maximinus, Decius, Valerian, Aurelian, and Diocletian). The last and most severe of these persecutions is commonly called the "Great Persecution" (A.D. 303-311). State-sponsored attacks on Christians ended with the "Edict of Milan," which legalized Christianity. It was signed by Constantine and his co-emperor Licinius in A.D. 313.

This book focuses on the lives of three Roman emperors — Nero, Domitian, and Constantine. They were key figures in the history of the early church and are all referred to in Scripture. Nero was the emperor to whom Paul appealed (and was eventually martyred under), Domitian was the villain in Revelation, and Constantine was the one who removed the "restraint" mentioned in 2 Thessalonians 2. Christians need to know about these emperors!

"If they persevered in their confession, I ordered them to be executed..."

Pliny to the emperor

NERO

Nero was the emperor of the Roman Empire from A.D. 54-68. He was a crude leader known for his extravagance and tyranny. Christians most remember Nero as a vicious persecutor of the early saints. He brutally tortured them to death for crimes they did not commit.

> **"The barbarities exercised on the Christians were such as even excited the commiseration of the Romans themselves. Nero even refined upon cruelty, and contrived all manner of punishments for the Christians that the most infernal imagination could design"** (*Foxe's Book of Martyrs,* p. 12).

Nero was born in A.D. 37. His birthplace was Antium, a town near Rome. His original name was Lucius Domitius Ahenobarbus. He was the son of Gnaeus Domitius Ahenobarbus and Agrippina the Younger. Nero's father died when he was three years old.

Agrippina married Emperor Claudius in A.D. 49. He was her third husband and she was his fourth wife. He was also her uncle. Claudius later adopted Nero as his own son, which meant that Nero took precedence over Claudius' own younger son Britannicus. Nero was tutored by the noted philosopher Seneca.

Nero married Octavia in A.D. 53. She was Claudius' daughter and his stepsister. It was an unhappy marriage that would eventually end in divorce and her execution.

> **"For Octavia, from the first, her marriage-day was a kind of funeral, brought, as she was, into a house where she had nothing but scenes of mourning"** (***Annals***, **14:63**).

Claudius died in A.D. 54. It is believed that Agrippina hired a woman named Locusta to poison a dish of mushrooms. This cleared the way for Nero, a teenager, to become the fifth emperor of Rome.

Though Agrippina exerted a great deal of influence over Nero early in his reign, her power soon waned. This led to an intense power-struggle that would ultimately bring their relationship to a tragic end.

Britannicus died in A.D. 55. It is believed that Nero hired Locusta to poison Britannicus at a dinner party in the palace. Nero attributed his stepbrother's violent reaction and subsequent death to epilepsy. This took care of a political rival, whom Agrippina had threatened to present as the true heir to the throne.

Nero's relationship with his mother continued to deteriorate. She was forced out of the palace and deprived of all royal honors, including bodyguards. Then he made several attempts on her life, one of which involved rigging a boat to sink with her on it. Exasperated, he had her killed by an assassin in A.D. 59.

A turning point in the reign of Nero came in A.D. 62. His trusted advisor Burrus died of illness and his mentor Seneca retired in frustration. They were replaced by Rufus and Tigellinus, who made little effort to restrain Nero's excesses and debauchery. In that same year, Nero divorced, banished, and then killed Octavia; and married his mistress Poppaea. Poppaea had been married to Otho, who would later become emperor. She bore Nero a child named Claudia in A.D. 63, but the girl died in infancy.

Seneca the Younger was a philosopher and statesman. He tutored Nero and later became his advisor. Seneca was forced to commit suicide for allegedly conspiring to assassinate Nero in A.D. 65.

A large section of Rome burned in A.D. 64 ("The Great Fire"). The fire lasted six days and left thousands homeless. A combination of summer winds, wooden buildings, and narrow streets contributed to the fire's massive devastation. Though Nero was at a country estate outside of Rome when the fire erupted, he returned to the city and offered assistance. Nevertheless, many suspected that he ordered the fire for his own building projects, and several sources report that Nero sang as he watched the city burn.

With suspicion mounting, Nero needed someone to blame for the fire. He found his scapegoat in the Christians. They were brutally persecuted in a public spectacle.

> **"Consequently, to get rid of the report, Nero fastened the guilt and inflicted the most exquisite tortures on a class hated for their abominations, called 'Christians' by the populace... Mockery of every sort was added to their deaths. Covered with the skins of beasts, they were torn by dogs and perished, or were nailed to crosses, or were doomed to the flames and burnt, to serve as a nightly illumination, when daylight had expired" (*Annals,* 15:44).**

This was the first state-sponsored attack on members of the church. The brutality was so severe that the people began to feel sorry for the Christians. Peter and Paul likely suffered martyrdom in the wake of this persecution.

Nero used the area destroyed by the fire to build an expansive palace complex ("The Golden Palace"), which included a huge statue of the emperor, elaborate decorations, pleasure gardens, and an artificial lake. It was impressive but not popular among the people.

As for his physical appearance, Nero was not exceptional. Suetonius described him as blemished and potbellied.

> **"He was about the average height, his body marked with spots and malodorous, his hair light blond, his features regular rather than attractive, his eyes blue and somewhat weak, his neck over thick, his belly prominent, and his legs very slender"** (*The Lives of the Twelve Caesars, Nero,* **51**).

Nero loved to sing, and began performing on stage in public. This was much to the chagrin of the people, who felt that he was an embarrassment to the throne. This led to scandal.

A famous conspiracy against Nero was devised and exposed in A.D. 65 ("The Pisoian Conspiracy"). Several distinguished men, led by a statesman named Piso, sought to "rescue the state" by killing the emperor. However, they were betrayed by a man named Milichus. This resulted in mass executions and forced suicides. Seneca and his nephew Lucan were among those who died. In that same year, Nero kicked his pregnant wife Poppaea to death in a fit of rage.

Nero married a third woman named Messalina in A.D. 66. She kept a much lower profile in public than her predecessor and outlived her husband. Otho later planned to marry her, but died before doing so.

The perverseness of Nero was extreme. He married a man named Pythagoras, whom he called his husband, and a man named Sporus, whom he called his wife. Sporus bore an uncanny resemblance to Poppaea and answered to her name.

> **"He castrated the boy Sporus and actually tried to make a woman out of him; and he married him with all the usual ceremonies, including a dowry and a bridal veil, took him to his house attended by a great throng, and treated him as his wife"** (*The Lives of the Twelve Caesars, Nero,* **28**).

Furthermore, Nero seduced married women, had romantic encounters with his own mother, and even devised a kind of game, in which he dressed in animal skins, sprang out of a cage, and attacked the private parts of men and women bound to stakes.

The deranged Nero finally lost control of his empire in A.D. 68. The senate voted to condemn him to death by flogging, but he committed suicide first. His private secretary Epaphroditus assisted him. (Epaphroditus was later executed by Domitian for failing to prevent Nero's suicide). Nero's last words were, "What an artist the world is losing in me." Nero was barely in his thirties.

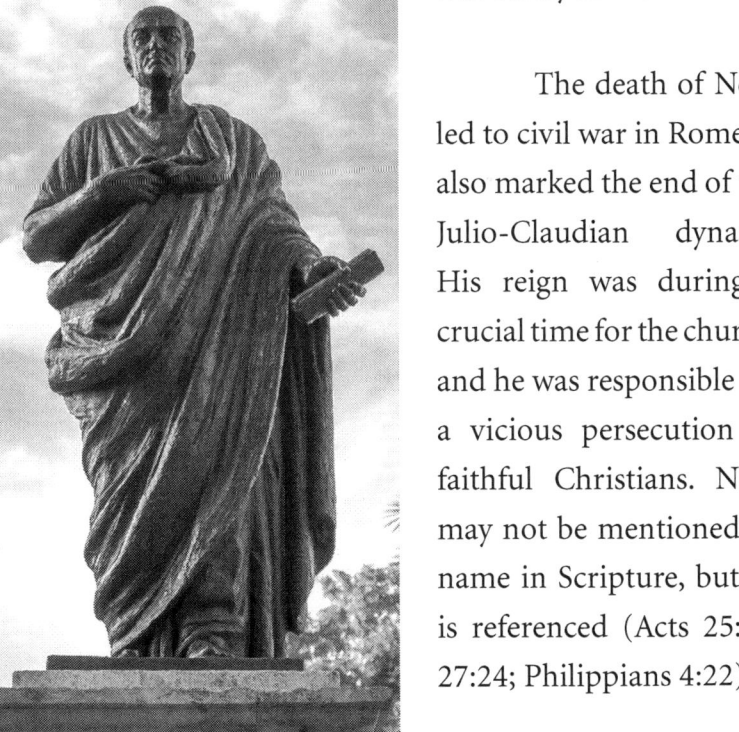

The death of Nero led to civil war in Rome. It also marked the end of the Julio-Claudian dynasty. His reign was during a crucial time for the church, and he was responsible for a vicious persecution of faithful Christians. Nero may not be mentioned by name in Scripture, but he is referenced (Acts 25:11; 27:24; Philippians 4:22).

Seneca

DOMITIAN

Domitian was the emperor of the Roman Empire from A.D. 81-96. He was a cruel and paranoid leader known for micromanaging all parts of the government and civil affairs. Christians most remember Domitian as a vicious persecutor of our early brethren, including John the apostle.

> "The emperor Domitian, who was naturally inclined to cruelty, first slew his brother, and then raised the second persecution against the Christians... Among the numerous martyrs that suffered during this persecution was Simeon, bishop of Jerusalem, who was crucified; and St. John, who was boiled in oil, and afterward banished to Patmos" (*Foxe's Book of Martyrs,* p. 13).

Domitian was born in A.D. 51. His birthplace was Rome. He was the youngest son of Vespasian and Domitilla. Vespasian was emperor from A.D. 69-79. Domitian's older brother, Titus, was also emperor from A.D. 79-81.

Domitian's youth and early career were spent in the shadow of Titus, who was highly regarded. The two brothers were never close, as is evidenced by the fact that Domitian hurried to the praetorian camp to be declared emperor while Titus lay dying. Many believe that Domitian poisoned his brother.

Domitian married Domitia Longina in A.D. 70-71. She was the daughter of a renowned general, Gnaeus Domitius Corbulo, whom Nero forced to commit suicide in A.D. 66. Domitia divorced her first husband to marry Domitian.

Domitian's only child was born in A.D. 80, but he died a few years later in A.D. 83. In that same year, Domitia was briefly exiled by her husband for reasons unknown. She was soon returned to the palace where she lived for the remainder of Domitian's reign.

Domitian was personally involved in every aspect of his administration. He implemented an ambitious building program, embarked on military campaigns, and managed the empire's finances. The Roman Senate's power was greatly diminished during Domitian's reign, for he viewed himself as the divine monarch.

"The abiding significance of his somber fifteen years as emperor is that a sharp advance was made toward complete

autocracy and monarchy" (*The Zondervan Pictorial Encyclopedia of the Bible,* Vol. 2, p. 155).

Domitian showed favor to his soldiers and increased their wages more than any previous emperor. However, he never acquired the military reputation of his father and brother. His triumphs were not as spectacular as theirs, and he was often criticized for his tactical and strategic decisions.

Domitian spent much time in solitude, which may have been the result of a lonely childhood. His mother died at a relatively young age and his father was often away, leaving Domitian in the care of others.

As for his physical appearance, Suetonius described Domitian as tall and handsome in his youth. He was, however, very sensitive about his hair loss as he aged.

> "He was tall of stature, with a modest expression and a high colour. His eyes were large, but his sight was somewhat dim. He was handsome and graceful too, especially when a young man, and indeed in his whole body with the exception of his feet, the toes of which were somewhat cramped. In later life he had the further disfigurement of baldness, a protruding

> belly, and spindling legs, though the latter
> had become thin from a long illness...
> He was so sensitive about his baldness,
> that he regarded it as a personal insult if
> anyone else was twitted with that defect
> in jest or in earnest" *(The Lives of the
> Twelve Caesars, Domitian,* 18).

Domitian was very paranoid. He did not hesitate to punish anyone he suspected of having divided loyalties, including family members. Some of his own kin were executed or exiled by the emperor.

Domitian imposed a state-religion upon the people in the form of emperor worship. Emperor worship involved burning a pinch of incense and declaring that Caesar was "Lord."

> "Once a year everyone in the empire had
> to appear before Domitian's magistrates
> to say *kaisar kurios,* Caesar is Lord, and as
> a testimony, to burn a pinch of incense to
> the godhead of Caesar. After this loyalty
> test, a written certificate good for one
> year was issued" *(The Royal Route of
> Revelation,* p. 13).

Obviously, this made life extremely difficult for Christians since they honored Christ as Lord (1 Corinthians 12:3), not Caesar. The consequences of that decision were often severe.

Domitian was assassinated in A.D. 96. The killer was a man named Stephanus, though he was aided by other conspirators. It is believed that Domitian's wife was involved in the plot.

Domitian's death brought an end to the Flavian dynasty. He was succeeded the very same day by Nerva. Domitian is not mentioned by name in Scripture, but he is certainly referenced in the book of Revelation as the great persecutor of God's church.

CONSTANTINE

Constantine was the emperor of the Roman Empire from A.D. 306-337. He was not the sole ruler, however, until he dispatched Maxentius (A.D. 312) and Licinius (A.D. 324) in civil wars. He is known for reforming the military, revitalizing the economy, relocating the capital, and reversing the persecutory policies of the empire toward Christianity.

Constantine was born in A.D. 272. His birthplace was Naissus, in the province of Moesia Superior. His original name was Flavius Valerius Aurelius Constantinus. He was the son of Constantius and Helena. Constantius was a Roman emperor and is sometimes known by his nickname Chlorus. Helena was a Bithynian woman of low social status.

Constantine's father left Helena to marry Theodora in A.D. 293 (some date this around A.D. 288-289). She was the daughter of Emperor Maximian. The marriage was politically motivated and resulted in Constantine having three half-brothers and three half-sisters.

Constantine had two wives. He was first married to Minervina (A.D. 303-307). They had one son (Crispus). He then married Fausta (A.D. 307-326), who was the sister of Maxentius and the daughter of Maximian. This marriage was also politically motivated. Constantine and Fausta had three sons (Constantine II, Constantius II, and Constans) and two daughters (Constantina and Helena). Constantine would later kill Crispus and Fausta.

Constantine is most known for his relationship to Christianity. He did many things to promote and protect the Christian religion during his emperorship, though that came with a price.

> **"Church and state were becoming closely intertwined. The church enjoyed the protection and patronage of the emperor, but in return it would have to deal with the authority of the emperor... Instead of persecuting the church, the emperor was telling it what to do. Constantine was the sole master of the Roman empire and, as far as he was concerned, this made him the sole master of the church too; he even called himself 'bishop'"** (*Zondervan Handbook to the History of Christianity*, pp. 77, 81).

Constantine claimed to have seen a cross of light in the sky with the inscription "In this sign, you will conquer" just

The Arch of Constantine next to Rome's Coliseum.

before the Battle of the Milvian Bridge in A.D. 312. He also said that Christ told him to use the sign against his enemies in a dream. Constantine took the advice and was victorious, resulting in his so-called "conversion."

It is important to note that this was not a pure form of Christianity or a Scriptural conversion. Constantine was not baptized until A.D. 337, as he lay on his deathbed. (Apparently he was sprinkled at that time. True baptism is a burial in water). Furthermore, Constantine retained the pagan title *Pontifex Maximus*, which emperor's bore as heads of their priesthood.

Though Constantine promoted and protected Christianity, it was not made the "state religion" in an official sense during his reign. That occurred later under Emperor Theodosius.

In A.D. 313, Constantine and his co-emperor Licinius issued the "Edict of Milan." The edict legalized Christianity. Below is an excerpt.

> **"Wherefore, as I, Constantine Augustus, and I, Licinius Augustus, came under favorable auspices to Milan, and took under consideration all affairs that pertained to the public benefit and welfare, these things among the rest appeared to us to be most advantageous and profitable to all. We have resolved among the first things to ordain, those matters by which reverence and worship to the Deity might be exhibited. That is how we may grant likewise to the Christians, and to all, the free choice to follow that mode of worship which they may wish... that no freedom at all shall be refused to Christians, to follow or to keep their observances or worship... that each one of the Christians may freely and without molestation, pursue and**

follow that course and worship which he has proposed to himself… that you may know we have granted liberty and full freedom to the Christians, to observe their own mode of worship" (*Eusebius' Ecclesiastical History,* pp. 372-373).

The edict, which also restored property that had been taken from Christians, was a stunning reversal of state policy. After all, this was just a few years after the "Great Persecution" (A.D. 303-311).

Though Christians had viewed Sunday as "the Lord's day" since the first century, for that was the day Jesus rose from the dead, Constantine made Sunday the official day of rest for the Roman Empire in A.D. 321. He issued a law prohibiting manual labor and judicial transactions.

"On the venerable day of the Sun let the magistrates and people residing in cities rest, and let all workshops be closed. In the country, however, persons engaged in agriculture may freely and lawfully continue their pursuits; because it often happens that another day is not suitable for grain-sowing or for vine-planting; lest by neglecting the proper amount for such operations the bounty of heaven

should be lost" (quoted from *History of the Christian Church,* III, p. 380).

In A.D. 325, Constantine convened the "First Council of Nicea." The meeting took place in the city of Nicea (in Bythinia) and included about 318 bishops. The doctrine of Arius and other controversial matters were discussed. Arius did not believe that Christ was equal to the Father, or of the same substance. Constantine bore the expense of all who came. The result was the "Nicean Creed."

> **"We believe in one God the Father almighty, maker of all things both visible and invisible, and in one Lord, Jesus Christ, the son of God, begotten by the Father, begotten — that is to say of the substance of the Father, God of God, light of light, very God of very God, begotten not made, being of one substance with the Father, by whom all things were made, both things in heaven and things on earth, who for us men and our salvation, came down and was made flesh, made man, suffered and rose again on the third day and went into the heavens and is to come again to judge both the quick and the dead, and in the Holy Ghost" (quoted**

from *History of the Church Through the Ages,* p. 42).

The council also set the day for Easter, a religious observance that first appears in the second century and is without divine authority.

> **"There is no indication of the observance of the Easter festival in the New Testament, or in the writings of the apostolic Fathers. The sanctity of special times was an idea absent from the minds of the first Christians"** (*Encyclopedia Britannica,* VII, p. 859).

One of the bishops involved at the "First Council of Nicea" was Nicholas, bishop of Myra. He had a reputation of gift-giving, such as putting coins in the shoes of those who left them out for him. He became the model for Santa Claus.

Constantine took part in settling doctrinal affairs, appointed Christians to high office, exempted the clergy from taxes, built basilicas, etc. This naturally led to a blending of church and state, which produced even more impurity in an already apostate form of Christianity. The church was socially strengthened but spiritually weakened. Its moral fabric eroded.

"These evil results may be summed up under the general designation of the secularization of the church... Christianity became a matter of fashion. The number of hypocrites and formal professors rapidly increased; strict discipline, zeal, self-sacrifice, and brotherly love proportionally ebbed away; and many heathen customs and usages, under altered names, crept into the worship of God and the life of the Christian people. The Roman state had grown up under the influence of idolatry, and was not to be magically transformed at a stroke. With the secularizing process,

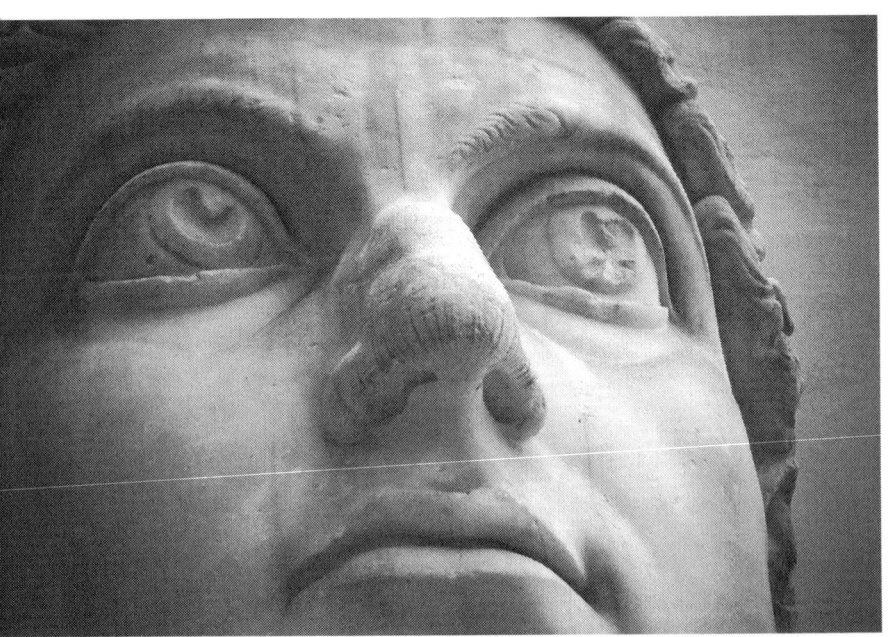

Constantine's bust

therefore, a paganizing tendency went hand in hand" (*History of the Christian Church,* III, pp. 125-126).

One of the most notable moments in Constantine's reign occurred in A.D. 324, when he moved the capital from Rome to the ancient site of Byzantium. It was called "New Rome" and then "Constantinople" in his honor. It had all the adornments one can imagine. The formal dedication took place in A.D. 330.

"The city was provided with all the amenities of Roman civilization — a forum, a basilica, public baths and the rest, as well as the trappings of the imperial court" (*Zondervan Handbook To The History of Christianity,* p. 73).

Constantinople (modern-day Istanbul) was a truly magnificent city. It bustled with activity and trade, and grew to perhaps 100,000 by the end of Constantine's reign.

In A.D. 331, Constantine commissioned Eusebius to produce fifty copies of the sacred Scripture for the churches of Constantinople. They were written in the Greek language. Some scholars believe that Codex Vaticanus and Codex Sinaiticus are two surviving copies.

Constantine had spared the life of Licinius after his defeat in A.D. 324. This was probably for the sake of his wife, Constantine's half-sister. However, the next year Constantine changed his mind and had Licinius executed (A.D. 325).

Constantine was greatly influenced by his mother, Helena, and she was even given the title *Augusta Imperatrix.* Helena claimed to be a Christian and visited Palestine. Tradition says that she discovered the actual cross of Christ.

Constantine was ambitious, organized, and very superstitious. Though he may have been one of the greatest emperors in Roman history, his impact on church history was for the worst. He secularized the church, paganized the church, extended the scope and power of councils, etc. He adopted his own model rather than trying to restore the one of the New Testament.

In A.D. 337, Constantine died near Nicomedia. He was baptized shortly before his death at the hands of Eusebius, bishop of Nicomedia. He had intended to be baptized in the Jordan River, but was unable to do so. Constantine's body was interned at the Church of the Holy Apostles in Constantinople. Sadly, he has been revered as "Saint Constantine" and the "Thirteenth Apostle" by some denominations.

Note: The apostle Paul spoke of an apostasy that would occur within church government, which would ultimately lead to the "man of lawlessness" taking his seat in the temple of God. That would not happen, though, until some "restraining force" was removed (2 Thessalonians 2:3-12). This writer believes that the restraining force was the Roman Empire. So long as it persecuted the church, there would never be the structure in place for the office of "universal bishop." However, when Constantine issued the "Edict of Milan" in A.D. 313, the church was no longer persecuted and its leaders were given state sponsorship. The restraint was removed. This eventually produced papal supremacy. Emperor Phocas crowned Boniface III "universal bishop" in the seventh century.

APPENDIX
(Christmas)

As we saw in our study of Constantine, the fourth century was a very significant time in church history. Christianity was legalized in the Roman Empire and began to prosper socially. The emperor proclaimed himself to be a disciple and did many things to promote his new religion. He made Sunday the official day of rest, appointed Christians to high office, exempted the clergy from taxes, built basilicas, financed excavation projects in Palestine, etc. It was now fashionable to be a Christian. That was not for the better, however, as the church was "secularized" and "paganized." A notable example of this was the celebration of Christ's birth on December 25th.

The celebration of Christ's birth on December 25th was not motivated by Scripture, but by paganism. It was an attempt to "metamorphose" pagan holidays into a Christian observance.

"The Christmas festival was probably the Christian transformation or regeneration

Left, Emperor Constantine offering Constantinople with St. Sophia Basilica to Virgin Mary (Holding the Christ Child) Byzantine mosaic art.
Faraways / Shutterstock.com

of a series of kindred heathen festivals —
the Saturnalia, Sigillaria, Juvenalia, and
Brumalia — which were kept in Rome in
the month of December" (*History of the
Christian Church,* III, p. 396).

The pagan festivals were immensely popular. They
were a highly anticipated time of banqueting and excess. That
fact surely influenced the decision to celebrate Christ's birth
on December 25th. Unable to stamp out the festivities, church
leaders tried to tame them and shift the focus to the Christian
"Son of God."

The New Testament does not tell us when Christ was
born or command us to celebrate the day of His birth. Rather,
it says to commemorate His death by eating the Lord's Supper
(1 Corinthians 11:23-29). In A.D. 245, Origen commented
that only sinners celebrated their birthdays in Scripture,
and cited Pharaoh and Herod as his examples (*Homilies on
Leviticus,* VIII). It was not until the fourth century that this
practice developed. Christmas was first celebrated at Rome
in A.D. 354, at Constantinople in A.D. 379, at Antioch in A.D.
388, and at Alexandria in A.D. 430.

ROMAN EMPERORS IN NEW TESTAMENT TIMES

Augustus.................. 27 B.C.–14 A.D.

Tiberius .... 14 A.D. –37 A.D.

Caligula................... 37 A.D. –41 A.D.

Claudius .... 41 A.D. –54 A.D.

Nero .... 54 A.D. – 68 A.D.

Galba....................... 68 A.D. – 69 A.D.

Otho........................ 69 A.D.

Vitellius .... 69 A.D.

Vespasian .... 69 A.D. – 79 A.D.

Titus........................ 79 A.D. – 81 A.D.

Domitian .... 81 A.D. – 96 A.D.

69 A.D. was a time of civil unrest known as the "Year of the Four Emperors"

KEY MOMENTS
IN CHURCH HISTORY

1st century — Church of Christ established; fire of Rome, resulting in first persecution by Roman emperors (64 A.D.); destruction of Jerusalem (70 A.D.)

2nd century — Distinction between bishops and presbyters (or elders); holy water introduced; infant baptism debated; first Easter observance

3rd century — Distinction between clergy and laity; sprinkling for baptism

4th century — The Great Persecution, which was the last and most severe in Roman Empire (303-311 A.D.); Christianity legalized in Roman Empire by Emperor Constantine (Edict of Milan, 313 A.D.); council convened to settle doctrinal issues (Council of Nicea, 325 A.D.), resulting in a human creed; Lord's Supper eaten on days other than Sunday; first Christmas observance; Christianity made the state religion of Roman Empire by Emperor Theodosius (380-381 A.D.)

6th century — John the Faster assumed title "universal bishop" for himself and was strongly opposed by Gregory the Great

7th century — Boniface III officially crowned "universal bishop" by Emperor Phocas (606-607 A.D.), resulting in papal supremacy; beginning of Islam; first instrument introduced by Pope Vitalian (666 A.D.)

11th century — Beginning of the Crusades (1095-1291 A.D.)

15th century — Printing press invented (Johannes Gutenberg), resulting in mass production of Bibles

6th–16th centuries — Dark Ages

16th century — Protestant Reformation

19th century — Restoration Movement

20th century — Discovery of Dead Sea Scrolls

Made in the USA
Charleston, SC
04 February 2014